How Eggworth Became An Easter Egg!

By Ann River

To eggveryone who
believed in this book!

One day not long ago me and my classmates went on a field trip to a farm. We were learning about our origins as hard boiled eggs. All of us were descended from chickens. In fact, my parents named me Eggworth, after my great, great, great grandfather... Eggworth the Great Chicken.

We also learned that all our ancestors were born in chicken coops just like this one.

On the farm I met a very nice rooster. His name was Cluck. He told me his job was to wake everyone up in the morning and to keep the chicken coop safe at night. Cluck said he was a "natural" at his job. I enjoyed learning about Cluck's profession, and I thought it might be fun to be a rooster.

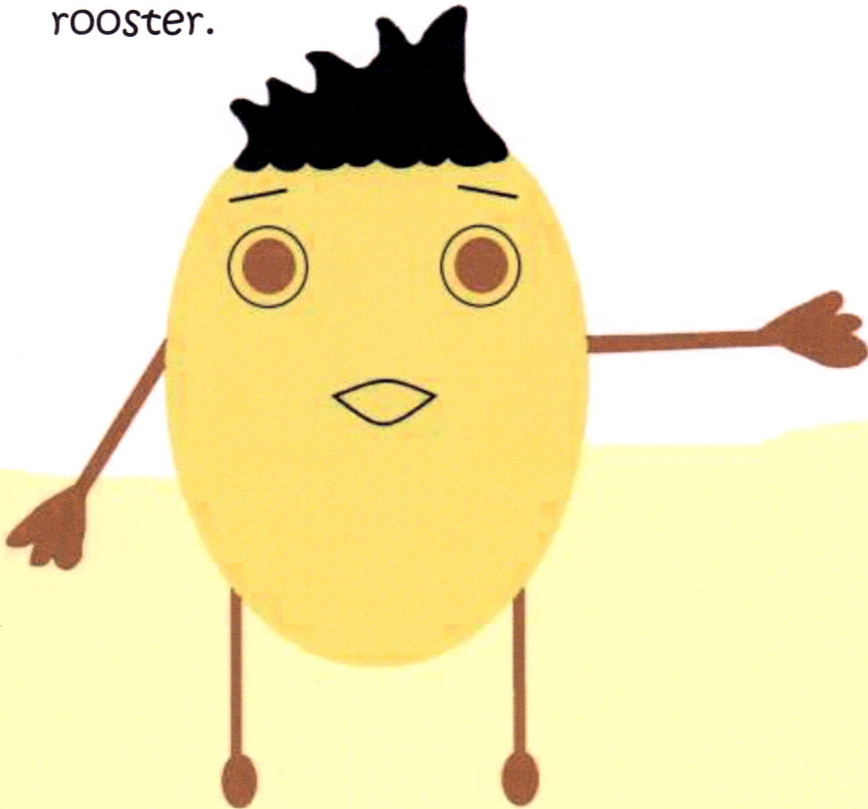

But I knew that hard boiled eggs can't become roosters. It was then that I started to wonder what I *would* do when I grew up? There were many different professions, but I wondered what I would be good at.

My friends Egford and Eglantine, had also gone on the field trip that day.

I told them about the rooster I met, and I asked them to visit my house after school. I wanted to talk to them about what they'd do when they grew up.

Later that day, I asked my friends which profession they thought they would be good at. Eglantine said she'd always wanted to be a decorator. Egford said he wanted to be a park ranger since he was always prepared to help.

Then my friends asked me what I thought I would be good at. I couldn't answer them, because I didn't know.

I realized it was time to put some serious thought into my future, especially since my birthday was in a few days and I would be another year older.

Even though I was still in elementary school, I knew jobs were important, but I'd never thought about *my* future profession before.

After my friends left, I started daydreaming about my future job. I imagined myself as a grownup. I wondered what I would be good at.

I imagined piloting a hot air balloon over the sea. I'd always wanted to try it. The beautiful views; the cool breeze from the ocean... *maybe* I'd be good at it.

Maybe not!
I realized that as an egg I've always been afraid of heights. I knew I'd probably land...SPLAT! Right in the *water!* Piloting is not a good profession for eggs.

If I were to land in the ocean,
I imagined I could row a boat.
Surely I'd be good at rowing a
boat.

But suppose there was a really big whale in my path. Hmm... I realized rowing a boat might not be a good choice for me either.

After that, I imagined the complete opposite of the ocean... the desert. I imagined myself working as a desert safari guide. I guessed it might be very hot there. Luckily, I'm hard boiled and the heat might not bother me.

But, suppose I came across a family of giant bugs marching across the sand? Most bugs are nice, but what if *these* bugs were hungry? Would a hungry bug eat an *egg*? I decided the desert wasn't for me at all.

Can hard boiled eggs be good at working in the snow? I imagined the arctic. It would be grand. Snow as far as the eye could see and no bugs in sight. I wondered what professions there were in the arctic. Maybe I'd just be a professional snowman maker.

I realized it might get too cold for a hard boiled egg in the arctic. It would be freezing! Hmm... can hard boiled eggs freeze?

If it got too cold in the arctic, I imagined my friend Egford might suddenly appear. He's always prepared for everything.

I knew he'd bring me a hat and a set of gloves. He would ask if the arctic was a good place for me and I would have to admit... it probably wasn't.

I imagined leaving the arctic. Even though I hadn't figured out what I would be good at; I knew my Birthday party would be in a few days.

I told myself that I would think about my future, after my party. But just thinking about my birthday *made* me think about my future... ugh!

A few days later, my Birthday arrived. I was very happy to see the balloons Eglantine brought for me. I thanked her.

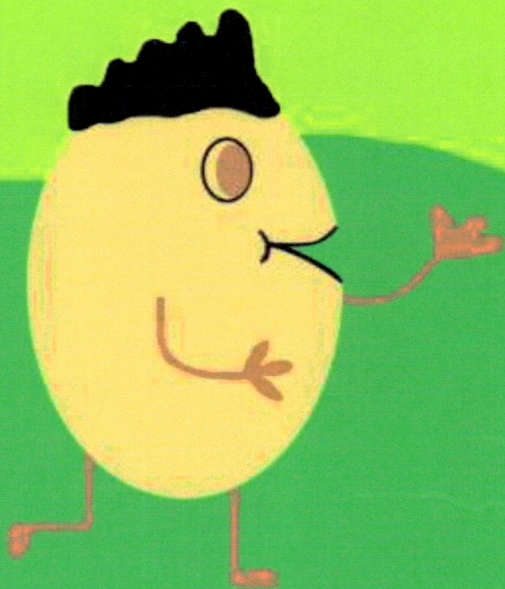

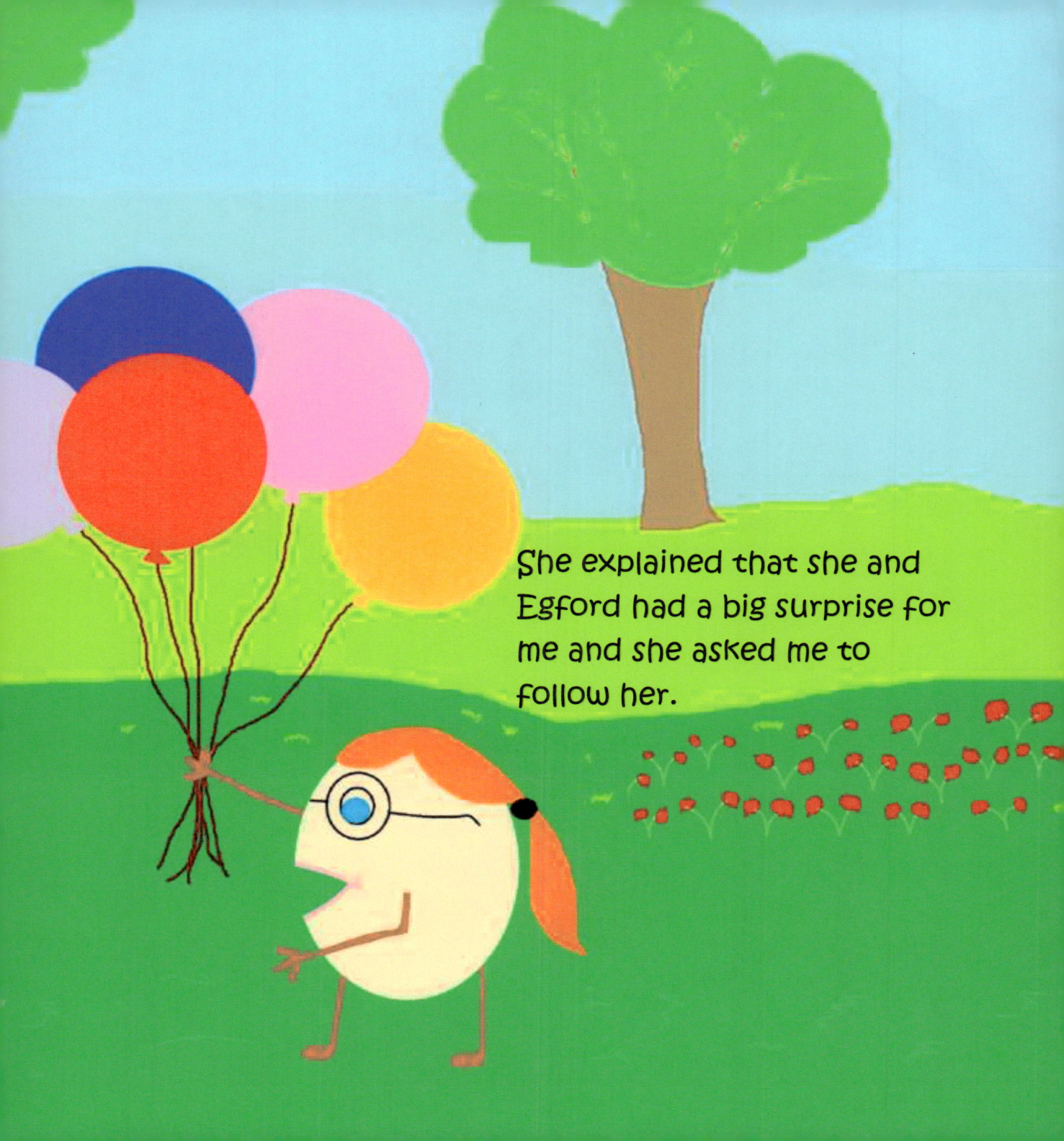

She explained that she and Egford had a big surprise for me and she asked me to follow her.

I followed her to a picnic table filled with presents and a cake. Egford was there. He wished me a happy Birthday! Then he asked if I figured out what I wanted to do when I grew up.

I told him I hadn't yet. Then he said, "Well, you know, I've heard that we hard boiled eggs make the best Easter eggs. Maybe you'd be really, good at that."

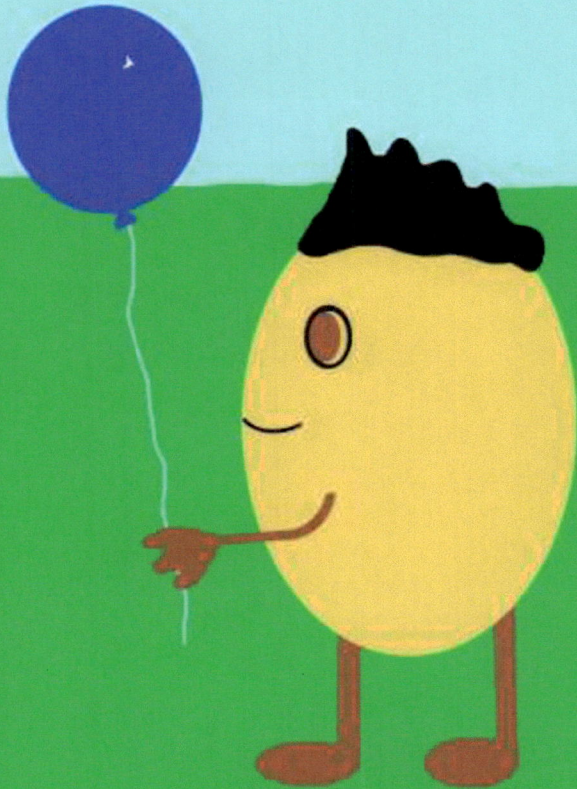

"That's right," said Eglantine, "not even roosters can become Easter eggs. The surprise is... We made an appointment at the Easter Egg Spa. We think you'll love it."

The next day we all went
to the spa.

We chose our hair color
first. Eglantine chose her
favorite colors.

I chose random colors, just to see how it worked. Egford said his hair color was going to be a surprise.

Next, we decided to
get a whole body "color
wash". Of course it
was only temporary
color.

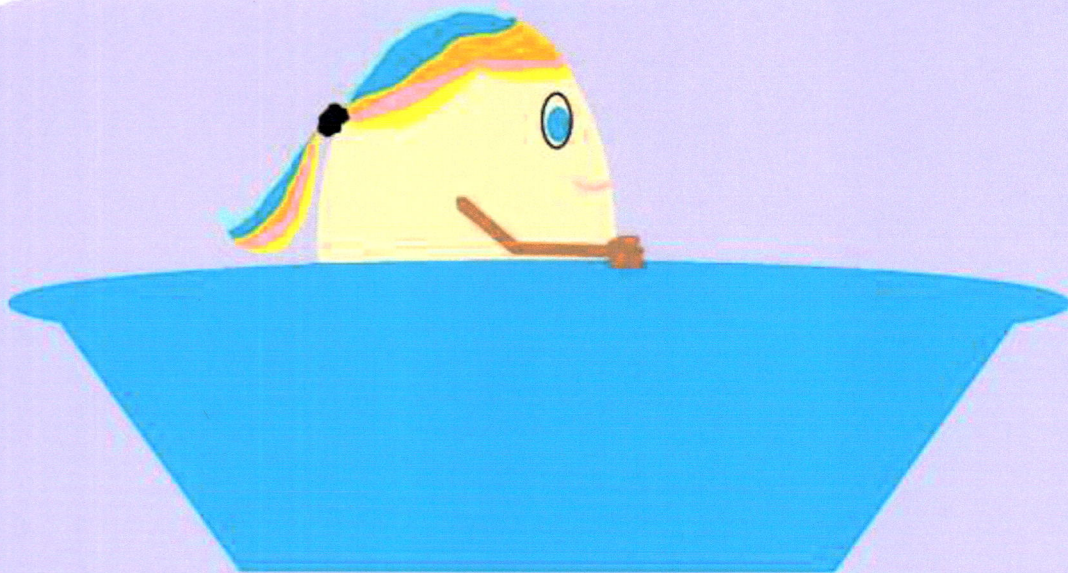

I fully enjoyed becoming a temporary Easter egg. I felt like I was a *natural* at it.

I knew that some hard boiled eggs grew up and became *fulltime* Easter eggs. The Easter Bunny was always looking out for new employees. Maybe I'd finally found my future job.

Eggworth

Egford

That night, I invited Egford and Eglantine to come over to my house for a sleepover. We watched our favorite TV show called, "Hard Boiled Not Scrambled".

Eglantine

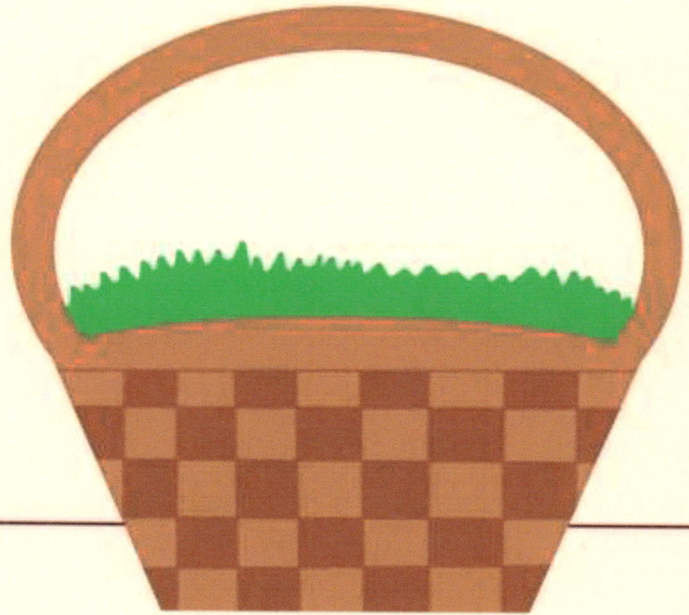

Easter was a week away and our temporary color would be gone by then. Although we weren't old enough to be real Easter eggs yet, it was fun to pretend.

After all of my imaginary travels, I'd finally figured out what I wanted to do when I grew up and that was...Become an Easter Egg!

Happy Easter!

Made in United States
Troutdale, OR
04/15/2025